ROBERT R. HERB:
A MAN OF MANY FACES

JOAN P. HERB

© 2024 JOAN P. HERB. All rights reserved.

No part of this book may be reproduced, stored in a retrieval system, or transmitted by any means without the written permission of the author.

AuthorHouse™
1663 Liberty Drive
Bloomington, IN 47403
www.authorhouse.com
Phone: 833-262-8899

Because of the dynamic nature of the Internet, any web addresses or links contained in this book may have changed since publication and may no longer be valid. The views expressed in this work are solely those of the author and do not necessarily reflect the views of the publisher, and the publisher hereby disclaims any responsibility for them.

Any people depicted in stock imagery provided by Getty Images are models, and such images are being used for illustrative purposes only.
Certain stock imagery © Getty Images.

This book is printed on acid-free paper.

ISBN: 979-8-8230-3543-9 (sc)
ISBN: 979-8-8230-3545-3 (hc)
ISBN: 979-8-8230-3544-6 (e)

Print information available on the last page.

Published by AuthorHouse 11/08/2024

CONTENTS

CHAPTER 1   EARLY YEARS..1

CHAPTER 2   ARMY SERVICE 7

CHAPTER 3   MARRIAGE, CAREER AFTER THE ARMY AND START OF
              FAMILY LIFE 13

CHAPTER 4   POLICE CAREER 19

CHAPTER 5   LOVE OF HISTORY AND REENACTMENT...................................33

CHAPTER 6   SELF-TAUGHT GARDENING AND PROPAGATION 43

CHAPTER 7   AN INTEREST IN AMERICAN INDIAN HISTORY AND ARTIFACTS......49

CHAPTER 8   POLITICS AND LEGISLATION 53

CHAPTER 9   THE HUNTSMAN AND NATURE LOVER 57

CHAPTER 10   FAMILY LEGACY: A HUSBAND, FATHER, GRANDFATHER AND
              GREAT GRANDFATHER 61

CHAPTER 11   EDUCATION, AWARDS AND ACHIEVEMENTS 65

EPILOGUE 71

CHAPTER 1

EARLY YEARS

ROBERT ROCCO HERB WAS BORN ON MAY 5, 1933 IN WEST NEW YORK, NEW JERSEY. HE WAS THE SECOND CHILD OF VIOLA AND JOHN HERB. HE, ALONG WITH HIS PARENTS AND OLDER BROTHER HERMAN, SPENT HIS EARLY YEARS GROWING UP IN FAIRVIEW, NEW JERSEY IN THE HOME THAT HIS FATHER BUILT.

ALREADY AT THE AGE OF THREE YEARS OLD, HE COULD NOT BE DISTRACTED EASILY FROM WHAT HE WAS DOING. HIS GRANDMOTHER WOULD TRY TO DISWAY HIM BY SAYING "BOBBY, DON'T DO THAT, YOU WILL MAKE NANA CRY". TO THIS HE WOULD REPLY "GO AHEAD AND CRY". DESPITE THIS ATTITUDE, HIS NANA WOULD LOVE BOBBY WITH ALL HER HEART.

AT AGE ELEVEN, BOB ALREADY SHOWED INTEREST IN PROTECTING OTHERS. HE BECAME A CROSSING GUARD DURING HIS ELEMENTARY SCHOOL YEARS.

IN HIGH SCHOOL, BOB BECAME INTERESTED IN SPORTS. HE RAN TRACK AND PLAYED FOOTBALL. HE WAS VERY GOOD LOOKING, SOCIALLY POPULAR, AND WAS VOTED "CLASS COMEDIAN". HE LOVED PERFORMING AND DOING IMPERSONATIONS.

DURING HIS HIGH SCHOOL YEARS, HE ALSO WORKED. HE TOOK A JOB AT PALISADES AMUSEMENT PARK AT A LEMONADE STAND. HE WOULD MIX THE FRESH SQUEEZED LEMONADE IN SILVER SHAKERS BEFORE POURING THEM INTO CUPS FOR THE

CUSTOMERS. THERE WERE A NUMBER OF TIMES THAT THE SHAKERS WERE FOUND TO BE STOLEN AND BOB SUGGESTED TO THE OWNER OF THE STAND THAT THE SHAKERS SHOULD BE PUT ON CHAINS IN ORDER TO DETER THEFT. IT WORKED! PROBLEM SOLVED BY OUR FUTURE POLICE OFFICER.

IN 1951, RIGHT AFTER HIS HIGH SCHOOL GRADUATION, BOB MET HIS FUTURE WIFE JOAN SETTEDUCATO. THEY DATED AND WHEN HE WAS DRAFTED FOR THE KOREAN WAR IN MAY 1953 AND SENT TO BASIC TRAINING, THEY DECIDED TO GET ENGAGED PRIOR TO HIS LEAVING OVERSEAS.

HIGH SCHOOL FOOTBALL

THE CLASS COMEDIAN

ROBERT R. HERB: A MAN OF MANY FACES   3

GRADUATION

BOB WITH HIS BROTHER HERMAN

JOAN P. HERB

ROBERT R. HERB: A MAN OF MANY FACES

JOAN P. HERB

CHAPTER 2

ARMY SERVICE

IN 1953, SHORTLY AFTER HE MET HIS INTENDED WIFE JOAN, BOB WAS DRAFTED INTO THE UNITED STATES ARMY DURING THE KOREAN WAR.

HIS INITIAL TRAINING WAS IN FORT DIX, NEW JERSEY FOLLOWED BY SUBSEQUENT TRAINING AT FORT MCCLELLAN, ALABAMA. AS HE WAS IN HIGH SCHOOL, BOB CONTINUED TO BE POPULAR WITH HIS FELLOW SOLDIERS. HE STILL DID IMPERSONATIONS AND NOW WOULD OFTEN SING WHEN THEY WERE OFF DUTY AND WENT OUT. HE WAS THEIR OWN "ELVIS".

PRIOR TO BEING SENT TO KOREA, HE WAS SENT HOME FOR SEVERAL WEEKS AFTER INJURING HIS ANKLE AT TRAINING IN ALABAMA. THERE WAS A CAST ON HIS FOOT. TYPICAL BOB, HE FIGURED OUT HOW TO TAKE OFF THE CAST WHILE HE WAS HOME SINCE HE "WASN'T WEARING IT" WHEN HOME. HIS MOTHER WAS SO UPSET THINKING THAT HE WOULD GET IN TROUBLE IF HE RETURNED WITHOUT THE CAST THAT SHE REPLASTERED THE CAST BACK ON BEFORE HIS RETURN!

ONCE HE RETURNED TO ALABAMA, BOB WAS THEN SENT TO THE 38TH PARALLEL IN KOREA. DURING HIS TOUR OF DUTY, BOB AND 2 OTHER SOLDIERS WERE CAPTURED OVER THE ENEMY LINE IN NORTH KOREA. A FEW MONTHS LATER NEAR THE

END OF THE WAR, THEY ALL WERE RELEASED IN EXCHANGE FOR THREE NORTH KOREAN PRISONERS HELD BY AMERICAN FORCES. FOLLOWING THE EXCHANGE, HE WAS ALLOWED "R&R" IN JAPAN. SHORTLY AFTER, HE WAS ABLE TO RETURN HOME TO THE U.S. IN MAY OF 1955.

Pvt. Robert R. Herb   **Pfc. Charles J. Orecchio**

Two Fairview Soldiers Hold Meeting in Korea

Two Fairview youths from the same neighborhood in Fairview, who had not seen each other for 1½ years met in Korea recently.

Pfc. Charles J. Orecchio, son of Mr. and Mrs. A. Orecchio, 349 Bergen blvd., Fairview and Pvt. Robert R. Herb, son of Mr. and Mrs. John P. Herb, 492 Jersey av., Fairview wrote home of their meeting.

Pvt. Herb had just arrived in Chankak, Korea, as a replacement and is attached to Co. 2 101st Signal Corps. Pfc. Orecchio is in the 872 QM Battalion, A Co., and will be leaving for home the end of this month.

JOAN P. HERB

ROBERT R. HERB: A MAN OF MANY FACES

JOAN P. HERB

CHAPTER 3

MARRIAGE, CAREER AFTER THE ARMY AND START OF FAMILY LIFE

After Bob returned home from Korea in May of 1955, as he promised before going to war, he married Joan (nee) Setteducato on October 16, 1955.

Newly married and now a civilian, Bob was employed by Great Bear Spring Water Company delivering water to offices in both New York and New Jersey. In order to advance in his job, he enrolled in Lincoln Technical School to learn plumbing. This would then enable him to install water coolers rather than just deliver water.

By 1957, Bob already had his first child, a daughter Theresa. He was expecting his second child in early 1959 (another daughter Patricia), when the New Jersey Division of Motor Vehicles posted a test for Highway Patrol officers. Since it had been Bob's secret desire to be in

LAW ENFORCEMENT, HE APPLIED. OVER 1000 APPLICANTS WERE RECEIVED BUT ONLY THIRTY-SIX OF THEM HAD PASSED THE EXAM. BOB WAS ONE OF THEM!

BOB ATTENDED THE NJ STATE POLICE ACADEMY FOR THE SIX WEEKS OF VIGOROUS TRAINING REQUIRED. HE WAS ONE OF THIRTEEN (FROM THE ORIGINAL THIRTY-SIX) WHO COMPLETED THE COURSE. HE WAS NOW ON HIS WAY TO A CAREER OF POLICE SERVICE AND ENFORCEMENT OF THE LAW.

BOB WOULD GO ON TO HAVE A THIRD DAUGHTER, BARBARA, IN 1963 DURING HIS POLICE CAREER, COMPLETING HIS FAMILY.

NJ DEPARTMENT OF MOTOR VEHICLES PATROL

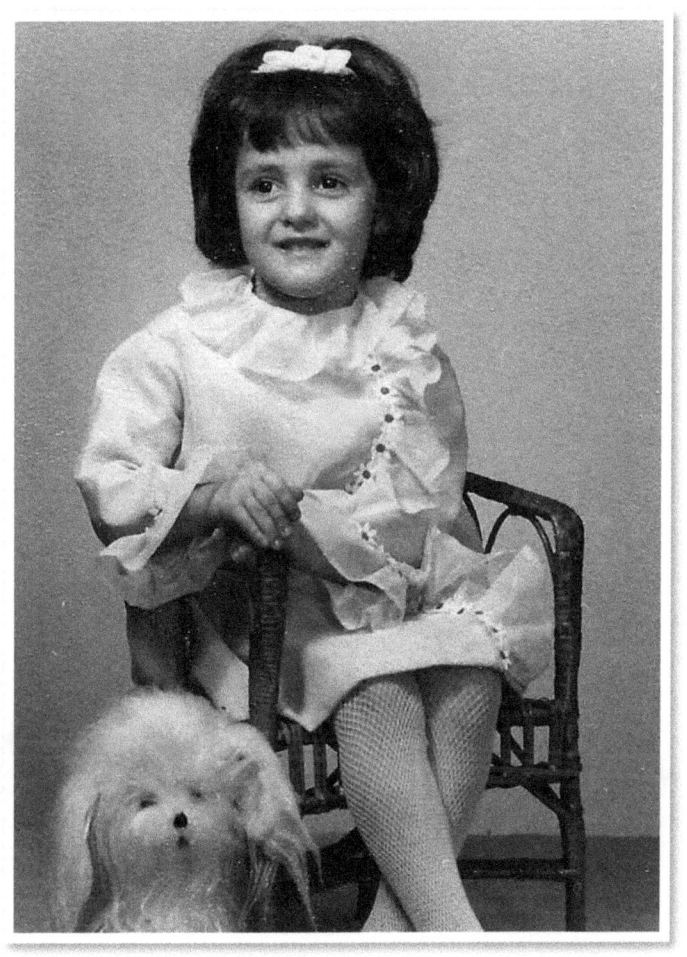

CHAPTER 4

POLICE CAREER

BOB'S FIRST TWO YEARS (1960-1962) WITH THE NEW JERSEY MOTOR VEHICLES HIGHWAY PATROL WERE QUITE AN INTRODUCTION TO HIS LAW ENFORCEMENT CAREER. PART OF THE JOB REQUIREMENT WAS TO GIVE DRIVING ROAD TESTS TO APPLICANTS AT THE DMV. ADDITIONALLY, IT WAS HIS RESPONSIBILITY TO RETRIEVE REVOKED DRIVERS' LICENSES AND GO OUT ON HIGHWAY PATROL ASSIGNMENTS.

WHILE ON PATROL (WHICH WAS BOB'S FAVORITE PART OF HIS JOB), HE ENCOUNTERED MANY DIFFERENT SITUATIONS. ONCE, HE STOPPED A MAN FOR AN EXPIRED REGISTRATION BUT ALSO DISCOVERED HE WAS DRIVING WITHOUT A LICENSE. HE TOLD BOB THAT ALTHOUGH HE HAD BEEN DRIVING FOR THIRTY-TWO YEARS, HE WAS NEVER ABLE TO OBTAIN A LICENSE DUE TO HIS INABILITY TO READ OR WRITE. BOB PRESENTED THIS INFORMATION TO THE MAGISTRATE DURING THE MAN'S HEARING, WHO THEN GAVE THE DRIVER A (SMALL) FINE BUT WAS ALSO ABLE TO PROVIDE HIM WITH AN ORAL TEST FOR HIM TO OBTAIN A PROPER LICENSE.

ANOTHER TIME WHEN ON PATROL, BOB OBSERVED A YOUNG MAN DRIVING WITH HIS FEET ON THE STEERING WHEEL. AFTER PULLING THE DRIVER OVER, HE APPROACHED HIM AND QUICKLY NOTED THAT THE INDIVIDUAL HAD NO ARMS! THE VEHICLE HAD BEEN SPECIFICALLY FITTED FOR THE DRIVER TO ACCOMMODATE HIS DISABILITY BY USING HIS FEET FOR DRIVING. THIS WAS A FIRST FOR THE YOUNG PATROLMAN.

HIS DAYS ON THE HIGHWAY PATROL WERE FAR FROM BORING. HE CAUGHT MANY DRIVERS SPEEDING, SOME SUSPECTS EVEN FLED BY FOOT AND BOB WOULD HAVE TO CHASE THEM, RUNNING AND JUMPING OVER BACKYARD FENCES TO APPREHEND THEM. ADDITIONALLY, THERE WAS A SIGNIFICANT INFLUX OF STOLEN TRACTOR TRAILERS DURING HIS TENURE ON THE HIGHWAY PATROL. BOB PROCEEDED TO RECOVER THE HIGHEST NUMBER OF STOLEN TRAILERS AND WAS EVEN GIVEN AN AWARD FOR HIS POLICE WORK.

IN 1962, THE STATE DIVISION OF MOTOR VEHICLES DECIDED TO DO AWAY WITH THEIR HIGHWAY PATROL DIVISION. BOB WAS THEN GIVEN THE CHOICE OF JOINING THE NJ STATE POLICE OR THE BERGEN COUNTY POLICE DEPARTMENT. HE MADE THE DECISION TO JOIN THE COUNTY POLICE SO THAT HE COULD CONTINUE TO RESIDE IN BERGEN COUNTY, ESPECIALLY SINCE HE WAS EXPECTING DAUGHTER #3 (BARBARA).

BOB ATTENDED THE NEW BERGEN COUNTY POLICE ACADEMY FOR TRAINING. HE WAS IN THE FIRST GRADUATING CLASS FOR THE DEPARTMENT AND WAS SELECTED PRESIDENT OF THE THIRTY-TWO PERSON CLASS AND SPOKE AT THE GRADUATION.

BOB CONTINUED TO BE A MODEL POLICE OFFICER FOR THE BERGEN COUNTY POLICE. IN 1970, HE RECEIVED A CITATION FOR OUTSTANDING POLICE WORK FROM THE DEPARTMENT.

IN 1974, BOB WORKED ON A MURDER CASE OF TWO TEENAGE GIRLS. THEY WERE MURDERED IN HUDSON COUNTY NJ BUT THEIR BODIES WERE DISCOVERED IN BERGEN COUNTY. SINCE BOB WAS FAMILIAR WITH HUDSON COUNTY, HE WAS ASSIGNED TO THE CASE AND WORKED WITH THEIR POLICE DEPARTMENT. THROUGHOUT THE INVESTIGATION, WHENEVER BOB WOULD HAND IN HIS FINDINGS, IT BECAME APPARENT TO HIM THAT SOMEONE WITHIN THE DEPARTMENT WAS EITHER CLOSELY INVOLVED OR COVERING FOR SOMEONE INVOLVED IN THE CRIME. HE SUSPECTED THAT THERE MAY HAVE BEEN TAMPERING WITH EVIDENCE AND QUESTIONING. ALTHOUGH HE HAD A STRONG SUSPICION AS TO WHO COMMITTED THE MURDERS, HE DID NOT HAVE ADEQUATE EVIDENCE TO BRING A CONVICTION. THE CASE WAS FINALLY CLOSED AS "UNRESOLVED".

FORTY YEARS LATER, A MAN IMPRISONED FOR THE MURDER OF ANOTHER YOUNG WOMAN CONFESSED TO THE KILLING OF THESE GIRLS. HIS CONFESSION DID NOT COMPARE TO THE EVIDENCE I KNEW BOB HAD. SADLY, SINCE BOB IS NOW SUFFERING FROM DEMENTIA, HE COULD NOT DISPUTE THIS CONFESSION

OR THE DETAILS THE MURDERER DESCRIBED REGARDING THE KILLINGS. I GUESS THE GUILTY WILL EVENTUALLY PAY. IF NOT NOW ON THIS EARTH, THEN IN THE HEREAFTER.

IN 1982, BERGEN COUNTY LED THE STATE IN DRUNK DRIVING DEATHS. A TASK FORCE (FUNDED BY THE FEDERAL GOVERNMENT) WAS LAUNCHED IN BERGEN COUNTY. AS PART OF THE PROGRAM, BOB HAD A MOTOR HOME CONVERTED TO A POLICE VAN EQUIPPED WITH A BREATHALYZER DEVICE TO TEST DRUNK DRIVERS WHO WERE STOPPED ON ROAD CHECKS. THESE ROAD CHECKS WERE PLACED IN VARIOUS LOCATIONS THROUGHOUT THE COUNTY AND WERE VERY EFFECTIVE. IN SOME LOCATIONS THAT WERE "ENTRY" POINTS TO NEW YORK WHERE TEENS WOULD GO TO DRINK, THE ROAD CHECKS PREVENTED MANY FROM DRINKING AND DRIVING AND SAVED MANY YOUNG LIVES. BERGEN COUNTY WAS NO LONGER A LEADER IN THE STATISTIC OF TEEN DRUNK DRIVING DEATHS. DUE TO THIS INITIATIVE AND GOAL OF REDUCING/ELIMINATING TEEN DEATHS, THE ORGANIZATION MOTHERS AGAINST DRUNK DRIVING (MADD) COLLABORATED WITH THE COUNTY POLICE AND INCLUDED AWARENESS CAMPAIGNS THAT MADE A DRAMATIC DIFFERENCE IN THE DEATH RATE OF TEENS.

DURING HIS TIME ON THE POLICE FORCE, BOB HAD MANY ENCOUNTERS WHERE HE ALMOST LOST HIS LIFE. ONCE AT THE END OF HIS NIGHT SHIFT ON PATROL, HE WAS RETURNING HOME VIA ROUTE 4 IN PARAMUS NJ. HE WAS IN THE RIGHT LANE PREPARING TO EXIT OFF THE HIGHWAY WHEN A MAN, WHOSE WIFE WAS FLEEING A NIGHTCLUB WITH HER BOYFRIEND, PURSUED THEM IN HIS CAR. HE RAN DIRECTLY INTO BOB'S CAR, DEMOLISHING IT, YET CONTINUED DRIVING AFTER HIS WIFE. MIRACULOUSLY, BOB HAD NO SIGNIFICANT BODILY INJURIES BUT SUFFERED AN IMMEDIATE CONCUSSION. CONFUSED, HE STARTED WALKING DOWN THE DARK HIGHWAY IN HIS DARK UNIFORM. HE WAS FORTUNATE TO AGAIN ESCAPE CATASTOPHE WHEN SOME FELLOW POLICE OFFICERS PICKED HIM UP AND TRANSPORTED HIM TO THE HOSPITAL. HE CALLED ME FROM THE HOSPITAL AND TOLD ME NOT TO WORRY – HE WOULD BE HOME SOON, "EVEN IF I HAVE TO JUMP OUT A WINDOW"!

THE SECOND INCIDENT I REMEMBER WAS WHEN BOB WENT TO THE CITY OF ENGLEWOOD TO CONTAIN RIOTS THAT WERE OCCURRING. DRESSED IN FULL RIOT GEAR, SOMEONE THREW A CINDER BLOCK FROM A ROOFTOP WHICH HIT BOB'S HELMET, CRACKING IT, AND SENDING HIM TO THE GROUND. AS A RESULT, HE SUSTAINED A SECOND CONCUSSION.

THE WORST EVENT WAS WHEN HE WAS PURSUING THREE BURGLERS/HOME INVADERS DOWN ROUTE 17 AS THEY CAME FROM THE ALLENDALE AREA. HE FOLLOWED THEM TO AN ACCESS ROAD BY TETERBORO AIRPORT WHICH ENDED IN A DEAD END. THE SUSPECTS THEN QUICKLY TURNED AROUND AND STARTED HEADING STRAIGHT TOWARD BOB. WHEN THEY SWERVED TO PASS HIM, ONE SUSPECT OPENED THE HATCHBACK OF THE CAR AND FIRED A SHOTGUN DIRECTLY AT BOB'S CAR, HITTING THE DOOR POST BETWEEN THE FRONT AND REAR DRIVER DOOR, RIGHT BEHIND HIS HEAD. IF BOB WAS NOT IN SUCH GOOD PHYSICAL SHAPE, HE WOULD NOT HAVE BEEN ABLE TO BEND FORWARD OUT OF THE LINE OF FIRE THAT WOULD HAVE BLOWN HIS HEAD OFF. SHAKING OFF THE BROKEN GLASS, BOB SAT UP AND CONTINUED TO PURSUE THE SUSPECTS DOWN ROUTE 17 AND THEN ONTO NJ ROUTE 3, ALONG WITH OTHER OFFICERS CALLED TO THE CHASE. ON ROUTE 3, THEY JUMPED OUT OF THEIR CAR WHEN THEY SAW THEIR OPPORTUNITY TO STEAL THE CAR OF A MAN WHO HAD STOPPED ON THE HIGHWAY AND WAS OUT OF HIS CAR. THEY CONTINUED DOWN ROUTE 3 TOWARD THE LINCOLN TUNNEL BUT EXITED ON TONNELLE AVENUE TO NORTH BERGEN. THEY THEN TURNED ONTO 42ND ST WHICH TURNED OUT TO BE A DEAD END. TWO OF THE THREE SUSPECTS RAN OFF IN ONE DIRECTION, BUT THE DRIVER, ATTEMPTING TO CLIMB A CHAINLINK FENCE, WAS APPREHENDED BY BOB. THE SUSPECT THEN NAMED THE OTHER TWO MEN INVOLVED AND THEY WERE LATER PICKED UP BY THE POLICE. THEY WERE CHARGED NOT ONLY WITH THE BURGLARY, BUT ALSO THE ATTEMPT OF MURDER ON BOB'S LIFE. BECAUSE OF HIS BRAVERY AND PURSUIT OF THE CRIMINALS, BOB WAS AWARDED THE COMBAT CROSS.

IN 1982, BOB WAS PROMOTED TO LIEUTENANT AFTER HE ACHIEVED COMING OUT FIRST ON THE TEST.

IN 1984, BOB APPLIED FOR THE TEST FOR CAPTAIN. UNBEKNOWNST TO HIM, HIS POLICE CHIEF AND A THEN CURRENT BERGEN COUNTY FREEHOLDER CONSPIRED TO HAVE HIM FAIL THIS TEST, FOR REASONS NOT CLEAR TO HIM. HIS CHIEF PERSONALLY TOOK HIM TO THE CIVIL SERVICE OFFICE PRIOR TO THE TEST. AT THE TIME, BOB DID NOT KNOW THAT THE SOLE REASON HE WAS BROUGHT THERE WAS SO THE PERSON WHO WOULD BE ADMINISTERING THE TESTS, WOULD KNOW WHO BOB WAS. THE DAY OF THE TEST, HOWEVER, THIS PERSON WAS LATE AND SO AN ASSISTANT GAVE OUT THE TESTS. WHEN SHE CAME IN AND SAW ALL THE TESTS WERE GIVEN OUT, SHE QUICKLY TOOK ALL THE TESTS BACK. SHE MADE BOB CHANGE HIS SEAT AND THEN GIVE OUT ALL THE TESTS AGAIN. WHEN THE RESULTS CAME IN AND BOB HAD FAILED, HE KNEW THAT SOMETHING WAS WRONG. HOW HE COULD FAIL THIS TEST WHEN HE ALWAYS CAME OUT NUMBER ONE FOR

BOTH THE SARGEANTS' AND LIEUTENANTS' TESTS? BOB PROCEEDED TO GO DOWN TO THE CIVIL SERVICE OFFICE TO INVESTIGATE THE RESULTS. TO HIS SURPRISE, HE WAS WELL ACQUAINTED WITH THE HEAD OF CIVIL SERVICE WHO SERVED ON GOVERNOR BYRNES' MOTOR VEHICLE COMMISSION ALONG WITH BOB. THE INVESTIGATION IDENTIFIED THE WOMAN WHO ADMINISTERED THE WRONG TEST TO BOB RESULTING IN THE FAILURE. SHE WAS THEN FIRED. MOST IMPORTANTLY, BOB WAS ALLOWED TO TAKE THE TEST AGAIN AND CAME OUT NUMBER ONE! AS A RESULT, HE WAS THEN PROMOTED TO CAPTAIN.

IN 1987, BOB WAS AT THE PINNACLE OF HIS POLICE CAREER. HE DECIDED TO RUN FOR SHERIFF OF BERGEN COUNTY AND WON. HE WAS THE FIRST POLICE OFFICER ELECTED TO THIS POSITION AFTER MANY YEARS IT BEING HELD BY POLITICIANS.

AS SHERIFF, BOB HAD HIS WORK AHEAD OF HIM. FOR INSTANCE, THERE WERE MANY RECENT ESCAPES FROM THE COUNTY JAIL PRIOR TO HIM TAKING THE POSITION. HE APPROACHED THE COUNTY FREEHOLDERS ASKING FOR FUNDS NEEDED TO DETER THE ESCAPES. POLITICS BEING POLITICS, HE WAS DENIED SO BOB TACKLED THE PROBLEM ON HIS OWN. HE PURCHASED RAZOR WIRE AND HAD IT INSTALLED AROUND THE PERIMETER OF THE JAIL. HE ALSO PURCHASED SIGNS THAT SAID "DANGER: ELECTRIC FENCE". THEN WITH THE ASSISTANCE OF AN ACTOR FALLING OFF A LADDER UPON TOUCHING THE FENCE, HE HAD THE INMATES BELIEVE THE SIGNAGE AND NO OTHER ATTEMPTS TO ESCAPE OCCURRED.

THE NEXT THING BOB WANTED TO CHANGE WITH THE JAIL WAS TO GIVE INMATES A PURPOSE EVERY DAY WHILE SERVING THEIR TIME RATHER THAN JUST SITTING AROUND. FIRST, HE IMPLEMENTED A PROGRAM WHEREBY A GROUP OF INMATES WERE ASSIGNED TO COUNTY ROAD CLEANUP. THIS ALLOWED THE INMATES TO HAVE SOME TIME OUT OF THE JAIL WHILE MAKING THE ROADS LOOK BETTER.

HE ALSO ALLOCATED INMATES TO HELP WITH COMMUNITY PROJECTS IN THE COUNTY. ONE WAS HELPING A CHURCH REPLACE ITS BELL. ANOTHER PROJECT WAS BUILDING A PLAYGROUND FOR ELEMENTARY CHILDREN IN THE CITY OF HACKENSACK. THEY ALSO HELPED RESTORE AN OLD COLONIAL DRILL HALL IN LEONIA, WHICH THEN WAS UTILIZED AS A MUSEUM AND A LIVE PLAYHOUSE.

THE INMATES WERE ALSO ASSIGNED TO PLANTING VEGETABLES IN A GARDEN ON THE JAIL PROPERTY WHICH WERE CONSUMED BY THE POPULATION. THEY ALSO GREW FLOWERS TO SELL ON MOTHER'S DAY, MAKE BIRDHOUSES AND DOLL HOUSES ALSO FOR SALE AND THE FUNDS WERE USED FOR THE COMMUNITY PROJECTS. THESE ACTIVITIES NOT ONLY MADE THE INMATES USEFUL TO BERGEN COUNTY

BUT GAVE THEM A SENSE OF ACCOMPLISHMENT AND, IN SOME CASES, LEARN A TRADE FOR WHEN THEY ARE RELEASED.

Lt. Herb Selected For Presidential Recognition Award

WITH PRESIDENT RONALD REAGAN

ROBERT R. HERB: A MAN OF MANY FACES

NJ GOVERNOR BRENDAN BYRNES' MOTOR VEHICLE STUDY COMMISSION

Bergen County police Lt. Robert Herb with the county's BATmobile.   Staff photo by Al Paglione

Beware the BATmobile

THE RECORD 9-1-83

A sobering influence

By Sue Warner
Staff Writer

Herb said the new van will allow police officers to [...] along the roadside, saving the time that had [...] to the nearest police [...]

[...]erly was used by Ber[...] is the latest ploy in a [...]de strike force to re[...] seven years, Bergen [...]ic fatalities. In that [...] on Bergen roads, and [...] percent, were drunk.

[...]rant, the strike force [...]orial Day weekend [...] on Bergen roadways. [...]od last year. So far,

Page 26—The Shopper, Tuesday, December 20, 1983

Lt. Herb honored

At a recent Remove Intoxicated Drivers regional conference, Freeholder Arthur F. Jones, public safety committee chairman, represented Bergen County in acknowledging Lt. Bob Herb, coordinator of the Driving While Intoxicated Strike Force. The R.I.D. New Jersey award was in recognition of Lt. Herb's efforts and leadership in implementing the D.W.I. Strike Force and the highly visible deterrent, the BATmobile.

FROM PAGE B-1

Bergen's 1983 traffic deaths total 38, which is behind Morris County's 47 and one more than Essex County's.

The strike force has so far stopped more than 10,000 drivers and made 170 drunken-driving arrests. Convicted drivers face a mandatory six-month to one-year license suspension and a fine of $250 to $400.

[...]t of the BATmobile, the Labor Day weekend will also mark a new stage of the strike force's crackdown, which Herb said will involve decoy roadblocks.

Herb said that starting this weekend, the strike force will occasionally plant bogus flares and a police car with its lights flashing on certain roadways. The real checkpoint, however, will be set up on a nearby roadway that intoxicated drivers would be likely to head toward to avoid arrest.

BERGEN COUNTY SHERIFF

JOAN P. HERB

SWEARING IN CEREMONIES BERGEN COUNTY SHERIFF

ROBERT R. HERB: A MAN OF MANY FACES

PRESIDENT RICHARD NIXON APPOINTED DEPUTY SHERIFF BY BOB

ROBERT R. HERB: A MAN OF MANY FACES

Sheriff Robert Herb in front of Leonia's drill house. He's using Bergen County Jail inmates to restore the historic building.

Inmates fix historic site

By Gregory Schutta
Correspondent

Drill hall is the last in the state

When it was built in 1859, the walls of Leonia's drill hall echoed to the voices of musket-toting militia who would soon be fighting in the Civil War.

But in 1989, a very different sort of army is occupying the Grand Avenue building.

A small troop of Bergen County Jail inmates is attempting to restore the fire-ravaged drill hall to the condition it was in at the turn of the century.

"We're hoping to restore it to a palatable condition, so that somebody will take it over and use it for a meeting hall or a restaurant, but protect the historic atmosphere," said Sheriff Robert Herb.

In order to do that, he said, the inmates will have to tear down a two-story addition that was gutted by fire in 1976 — one year before the drill hall was placed on the state and federal registers of historic places — and rebuild it with wood from the same era.

"Because this is a historic site, we have to use pre-1920 wood, which had the same full cut as the wood used in the original construction," Herb said. He is looking to get the wood from developers or the Department of Transportation, as they tear down old buildings.

Once the addition is demolished, the inmates will repair the roof, and then turn their attention to restoring interior fixtures such as the original musket racks and large candle chandeliers.

Herb said that he hopes to have the building restored by the fall.

The sheriff is a history buff who has taken part in many Revolutionary War reenactments, including that of George Washington's famous retreat from Fort Lee to Trenton.

"We're the last train out for this old building, which is the last Civil War-era drill hall in the state," Herb said. "Since it's a historic site, it couldn't be torn down, but a lot of people were praying it would fall so it could be replaced with housing or some other ratable."

Indeed, there have been numerous attempts to remove the site from the historic rolls since it was deeded to the borough in 1980 for one dollar.

Most recently, in 1987, the council looked into replacing the building with low- and moderate-income housing or a senior citizen housing complex. But the removal process was deemed too difficult, and the plan was dropped.

When it was originally constructed, the drill hall served as headquarters for Company K of the 22nd Regiment of the New Jersey Militia, more commonly known as the

See **DRILL** Page 5

CHAPTER 5

LOVE OF HISTORY AND REENACTMENT

THE U.S. BICENTENNIAL WAS IN THE YEAR 1976. BOB, BEING A GREAT HISTORY BUFF, THOUGHT THAT A WONDERFUL WAY TO CELEBRATE WAS TO RE-ENACT GEORGE WASHINGTON'S RETREAT THAT OCCURRED 200 YEARS AGO. THE RETREAT WAS ACROSS THE STATE OF NEW JERSEY FROM FORT LEE TO TRENTON. THIS WOULD ENABLE ADULTS AND CHILDREN TO SEE HISTORY "LIVE".

BOB APPROACHED THE BERGEN COUNTY CULTURAL AND HERITAGE COMMITTEE WITH HIS IDEA SINCE THEY WERE OVERSIGHT FOR ALL BICENTENNIAL EVENTS IN THE COUNTY. THEY REFUSED TO SUPPORT OR FUND BOB'S PROPOSITION AND HE WAS TOLD THAT HE SHOULD PURSUE IT ON HIS OWN. OF COURSE, BOB SOUGHT ANOTHER WAY FOR HIS IDEA TO COME TO FRUITION. HE THEN WENT TO THE COUNTY FREEHOLDERS AND TOLD THEM THAT HE WOULD NOT NEED ANY FUNDS FOR THE RETREAT BUT WOULD NEED SUPPORT FOR THE FIVE HOUR PROGRAM AT THE COUNTY COURTHOUSE. THE FUNDS WOULD PAY FOR THE WEST POINT BAND AND THE NEWARK BOYS CHOIR. THEY AGREED.

BOB ENLISTED THE HELP AND SUPPORT OF THE THIRTEEN TOWNS THAT THE RETREAT EVENT WOULD MARCH THROUGH. FOR EXAMPLE, HE ASKED THE TOWNS

TO DONATE OLD STREET SIGNS. BOB THEN TOOK THE SIGNS TO THE BERGEN TECHNICAL SCHOOL IN HACKENSACK AFTER THE FACULTY AND STUDENTS AGREED TO REPAINT THEM WITH THE RETREAT LOGO. THESE SIGNS WERE PLACED ALONG THE ACTUAL RETREAT ROUTE AND ARE STILL INTACT TODAY.

HISTORICALLY, THE RETREAT MARCH WAS THE EXACT ROUTE THAT GENERAL WASHINGTON TOOK IN 1776 WHEN HE RETREATED FROM LORD CORNWALLIS' BRITISH ARMY AS THEY ENTERED NEW JERSEY. SINCE THE RETREAT WAS A SOLEMN EVENT PAYING TRIBUTE TO THE MEN WHO MADE UP THE CONTINENTAL ARMY, BOB REQUESTED THAT THERE BE NO BANDS, FLOATS, MOTOR VEHICLES OR ANY SIGN OF COMMERCIALISM. ONLY A COLONIAL FIFE AND DRUM UNIT PROVIDED MUSIC. ALL THIRTEEN TOWNS IN BERGEN COUNTY, ALONG WITH THE VARIOUS COUNTIES IN NEW JERSEY WERE INVITED TO PARTICIPATE BY MARCHING IN COLONIAL DRESS ALONG WITH THE FRANCIS MERRION BRIGADE AND THE ROBERT ERSKIN MILITIA. APPROXIMATELY ONE THOUSAND UNIFORMED MILITIA FROM UP AND DOWN THE NEW JERSEY COAST PARTICIPATED. THE RETREAT TRAVELLED SEVENTY-EIGHT MILES IN FIVE WEEKENDS FROM FORT LEE TO TRENTON AND REACHED THE MEMORIAL BUILDING IN TRENTON ON DECEMBER 19, 1976.

IN RECOGNITION FOR COORDINATING AND PERSONALLY LEADING THE MARCH, BOB WAS COMMISSIONED AN HONORARY COLONEL RANK IN THE NEW JERSEY MILITIA. THE RETREAT ITSELF WAS NAMED AN OFFICIAL BICENTENNIAL EVENT AND WAS ENTERED INTO THE NEW JERSEY ARCHIVES IN TRENTON.

AFTER THE SUCCESS OF THE RETREAT, BOB CONTINUED TO ORGANIZE AND PARTICIPATE IN OTHER EVENTS. FIRST, HE WAS INVOLVED IN THE COMMEMORATIVE EVENT IN RIVERDALE, NEW JERSEY TO HONOR THE MEMORY OF CONTINENTAL SOLDIERS WHO WERE MASSACRED BY BRITISH FORCES ON SEPTEMBER 27, 1778. THIS WAS KNOWN AS "BAYLOR MASSACRE". IN 1779, THE BRITISH FORCES ATTACKED THE PATRIOTS LED BY MAJOR LIGHT HORSE HARRY LEE AT FORT PAULIS HOOK. AS A RESULT OF THIS BATTLE, THE BRITISH LOST MOST OF THE CONTROL OVER THE STATE OF NEW JERSEY. BOB COORDINATED THIS RE-ENACTMENT WITH JERSEY CITY IN 1979. ANOTHER LOOK AT HISTORY THANKS TO BOB.

THE FINAL AND MOST SPECTACULAR REENACTMENT BOB COORDINATED WAS THE TRIAL OF MAJOR ANDRE. ANDRE WAS A MAJOR FOR THE BRITISH ARMY WHO MET WITH THE INFAMOUS MILITIA GENERAL BENEDICT ARNOLD. ARNOLD HAD OBTAINED THE PLANS FOR THE DEFENSE OF THE FORT AT WEST POINT ON THE HUDSON RIVER AND WAS WILLING TO GIVE THOSE PLANS TO THE BRITISH.

STRATEGICALLY, THIS FORT WOULD PREVENT THE BRITISH ARMY FROM HEADING NORTH TOWARD THE NEW ENGLAND COLONIES AND CANADA.

THE REENACTMENT STARTED WITH THE INITIAL MEETING OF ARNOLD AND ANDRE IN HAVERSTRAW, NEW YORK. MAJOR ANDRE WAS TRANSPORTED UP THE HUDSON TO HAVERSTRAW ON A SLOOP "THE VULTURE" (ACQUIRED FROM THE MARITIME MUSEUM FOR THE EVENT). THE SLOOP THEN DROPPED ANCHOR IN HAVERSTRAW AND A WHALE BOAT BROUGHT HIM TO SHORE WHERE HE WAS MET BY GENERAL ARNOLD. FROM HAVERSTRAW, THEY RODE ON HORSEBACK TO THE OLD TREASON HOUSE IN WEST HAVERSTRAW WHERE THEY STAYED THE NIGHT. THE NEXT MORNING, MAJOR ANDRE WAS RETURNING WITH THE WEST POINT DEFENSE PLANS TO SHARE WITH THE BRITISH WHEN HE WAS CAPTURED BY MILITIA MEN, BROUGHT TO TARRYTOWN, AND THEN PUT ON TRIAL IN TAPPAN. HE WAS THEN FOUND GUILTY AND SENTENCED TO DEATH BY HANGING. THE TREASONOUS GENERAL ARNOLD, HOWEVER, NEVER STOOD TRIAL AS HE ESCAPED TO THE BRITISH FORCES AND WAS PLACED IN THE KINGS ARMY.

THE REENACTMENT OF THE MEETING IN HAVERSTRAW, CAPTURE, AND TRIAL AND EXECUTION OF MAJOR ANDRE WAS COORDINATED BY BOB. HE EVEN SOUGHT OUT TWO OF MAJOR ANDRE'S DESCENDENTS AND INVITED THEM TO THE EVENT. ONE CAME FROM AUSTRALIA AND THE OTHER DESCENDENT WAS ACTUALLY IN THE BRITISH ARMY AT THE TIME OF THE RE-ENACTMENT. THEY WERE BOTH VERY APPRECIATIVE OF THE COMMEMORATION OF THEIR ANCESTOR AND BEING INVITED TO THE EVENT.

AS YOU MAY SUMISE, THESE PROGRAMS WERE MONUMENTAL EVENTS THAT REQUIRED NOT ONLY ORGANIZATION, BUT MANY PEOPLE "BEHIND THE SCENES" THAT CONTRIBUTED TO THE SUCCESS OF THESE PROJECTS. IN ADDITION TO ATTENDING THE EVENTS, MY CONTRIBUTION WAS DESIGNING AND CONSTRUCTING THREE DIFFERENT COLONIAL UNIFORMS FOR BOB. I WORKED TO MAKE THEM AS AUNTHENTIC AS POSSIBLE AND AS YOU CAN SEE IN THE IMAGES THAT FOLLOW, HE LOOKED THE PART HE PLAYED AT EACH REENACTMENT.

NJ STATEWIDE BICENTENNIAL REENACTMENT

JOAN P. HERB

ROBERT R. HERB: A MAN OF MANY FACES 37

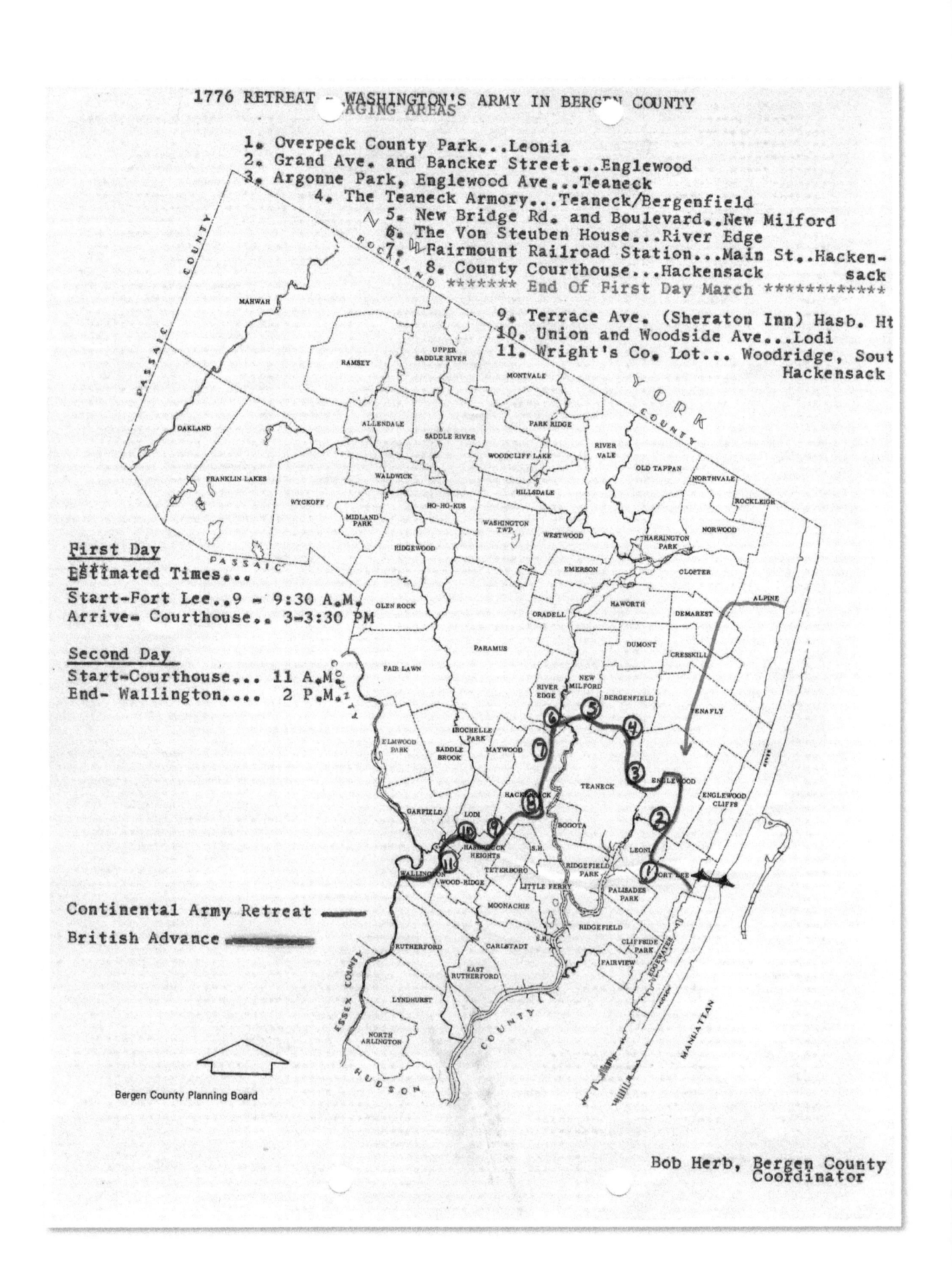

1776 RETREAT - WASHINGTON'S ARMY IN BERGEN COUNTY

STAGING AREAS

1. Overpeck County Park...Leonia
2. Grand Ave. and Bancker Street...Englewood
3. Argonne Park, Englewood Ave...Teaneck
4. The Teaneck Armory...Teaneck/Bergenfield
5. New Bridge Rd. and Boulevard..New Milford
6. The Von Steuben House...River Edge
7. Fairmount Railroad Station...Main St..Hackensack
8. County Courthouse...Hackensack

******* End Of First Day March ************

9. Terrace Ave. (Sheraton Inn) Hasb. Ht
10. Union and Woodside Ave...Lodi
11. Wright's Co. Lot... Woodridge, Sout Hackensack

First Day
Estimated Times...
Start-Fort Lee..9 - 9:30 A.M.
Arrive- Courthouse.. 3-3:30 PM

Second Day
Start-Courthouse... 11 A.M.
End- Wallington.... 2 P.M.

Continental Army Retreat ———
British Advance ═══════

Bergen County Planning Board

Bob Herb, Bergen County Coordinator

BATTLE OF PAULUS HOOK REENACTMENT

Bergen police officer leads 1779 reenactment

BERGEN NEWS
8-8-79

The Citizen's Committee For The Bicentennial Celebration Of The Battle Of Paulus Hook appointed Bob Herb, county police detective sergeant and Maywood councilman, as coordinator for the battle reenactment to be held Saturday, August 18 at 7 p.m. in Liberty State Park (Turnpike Exit 14B), Jersey City.

Paulus Hook was a British fort in the Revolutionary War, when on August 19, 1779, American Maj. Lighthorse Harry Lee led an expedition from River Edge and back after successfully capturing the fort.

Joining with Jersey City (which was part of Bergen County until 1840), the Bergen County Historical Society is holding the encampment of Major Lee at the Steuben House in River Edge that weekend. From that location the troops will travel to Jersey City and participate in the battle as originally done 200 years before.

Herb was the coordinator of the 1976 reenactment of Washington's Army Retreat From Fort Lee, the Baylor Massacre At River Vale in 1978, and will coordinate next year's reenactment of the spy trial and execution of British Major Andre at Tappan.

Holy Name accreditated

Holy Name Hospital, Teaneck, has again been

BOB HERB

Dick Braisted, a captain in Van Buskirk's Loyalists, left, crosses swords with Bob Herb, a New Jersey Militia colonel, at Paulus Hook. The two Revolutionary War buffs will be among those participating in the reenactment of the Battle of Paulus Hook, Saturday at 7 p.m. at Liberty State Park, Jersey City.

BAYLOR MASSACRE REENACTMENT

ROBERT R. HERB: A MAN OF MANY FACES

JOAN P. HERB

CAPTURE AND TRIAL OF MAJOR ANDRE

JOAN P. HERB

CHAPTER 6

SELF-TAUGHT GARDENING AND PROPAGATION

BOB WAS VERY DIVERSIFIED IN HIS INTEREST IN VARIOUS SUBJECTS. AS ALWAYS, HE GAVE ONE HUNDRED PERCENT TO WHATEVER HE DID. HE LOVED GARDENING AND ESPECIALLY GROWING HIS OWN VEGETABLES FOR OUR FAMILY. HE WOULD GROW TOMATOES, CUCUMBERS, BELL PEPPERS, RED AND GREEN LETTUCES, ZUCCHINI, AND GREEN BEANS. HE WOULD SPEND MUCH OF HIS SPARE TIME WEEDING AND MULCHING THE GARDEN, WHICH RESULTED IN THE MOST WONDERFUL CROPS WE ALL WOULD ENJOY.

HE ALSO LOVED GROWING FLOWERS AND FLOWERING SHRUBS WHICH COULD BE SEEN THROUGHOUT OUR LANDSCAPING. HE PLANTED DAFFODILS, ROSES, AZALEAS, LILIES, IRISES, ROSE OF SHARON, AND HYDRANGEAS, ALL WHICH HE LEARNED TO PROPAGATE. HE WOULD EVEN PUT SEVERAL OF THE PLANTS HE PROPAGATED IN POTS SO THAT OUR CHILDREN COULD PLANT THEM ON THEIR PROPERTIES AS WELL.

BOB ALSO BECAME INTERESTED IN GRAFTING APPLE TREES. HE TAUGHT HIMSELF THE TECHNIQUE WHEREBY HE WOULD TAKE A BRANCH OR SCION OF ONE TYPE OF APPLE (MOSTLY GRANNY SMITH, NORTHERN SPY, OR MCINTOSH) AND THEN

GRAFT THE SCION ONTO THE BRANCH OF ANOTHER TYPE OF APPLE TREE (A RED DELICIOUS TREE). WHEN THE NEW BRANCH TOOK AND THRIVED, USUALLY BY ABOUT TWO YEARS LATER, NEW APPLES WHICH WERE HYBRIDS OF THE ORIGINAL APPLES WOULD SUCCESSFULLY PROPAGATE. WHAT DELICIOUS APPLESAUCE ALL THESE VARIETIES OF APPLES MADE!

BOB FELT THAT HIS SUCCESS WITH THIS TECHNIQUE SHOULD BE SHARED. HE HAD ENLISTED HIS SON-IN-LAW TO DO THE GRAFTING, TOOK PICTURES OF THE PROCESS, AND DEVELOPED A SLIDE PRESENTATION WHICH HE TOOK "ON THE ROAD" TO VARIOUS GARDEN CLUBS. HE FELT THAT GRAFTING WAS A LOST CRAFT OVER THE YEARS AND BY TEACHING OTHERS, THERE WOULD BE NEW INTEREST IN THE TECHNIQUE.

BOB ALSO WAS INTERESTED IN THE CONSERVATION OF TREES IN OUR FORESTS. WHEN A CATEPILLAR BLIGHT HAD DESTROYED MANY TREES IN THE NORTHEAST AND SPECIFICALLY ON HIS PARENTS' SIXTY-TWO ACRE FARM IN PENNSYLVANIA, BOB PERSONALLY OBTAINED TREES FROM THE ARBOR DAY FOUNDATION TO PLANT IN THE DEVASTATED FOREST. HE HAD WELL OVER ONE HUNDRED TREES THAT HE PLANTED AND WITHIN A FEW YEARS, THEY WERE GROWING AND REPLENISHING THE FOREST.

APPLE TREE GRAFTING

APPLE TREE WITH FOUR DIFFERENT VARIETIES OF APPLES

JOAN P. HERB

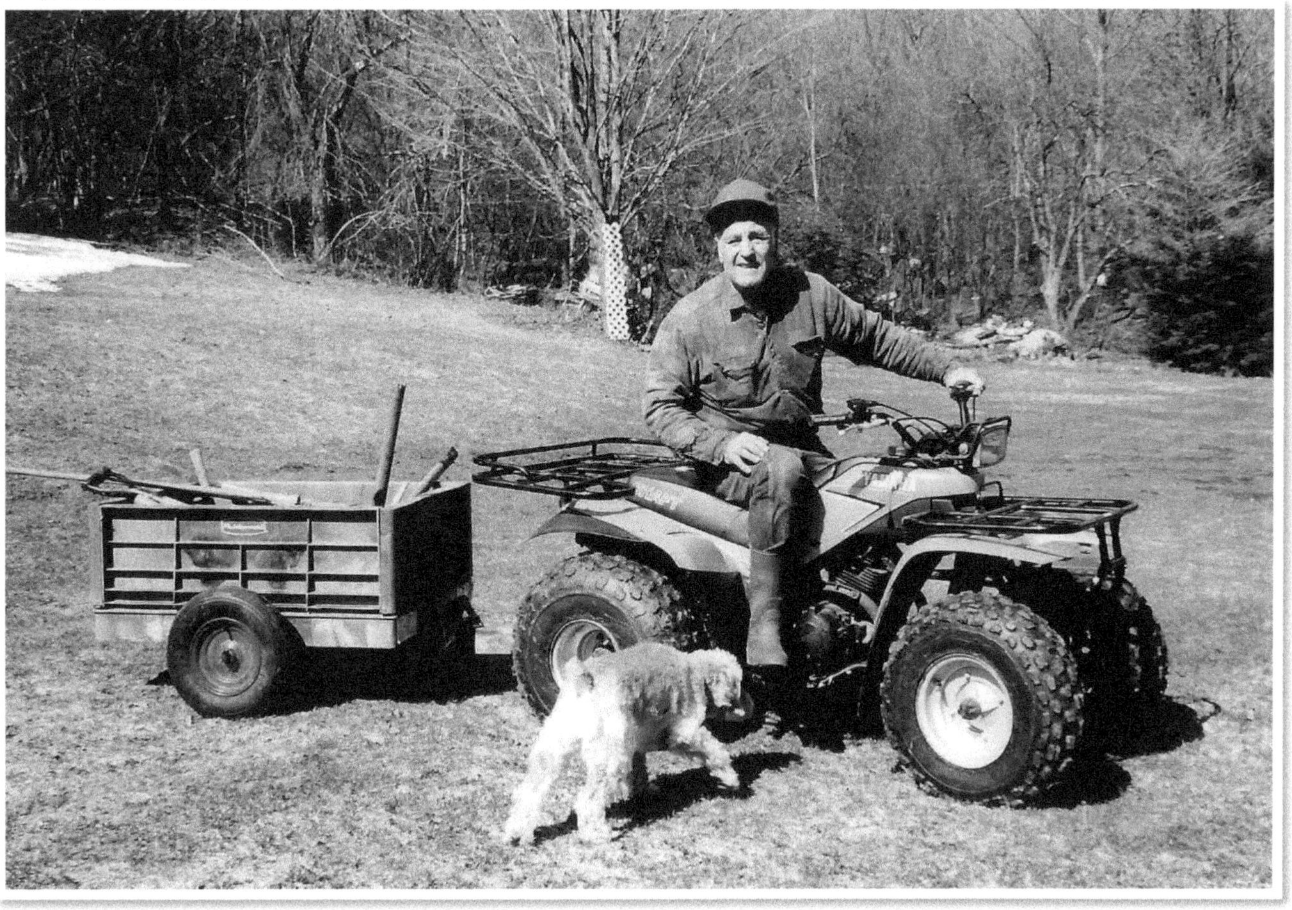

CHAPTER 7

AN INTEREST IN AMERICAN INDIAN HISTORY AND ARTIFACTS

BOB HAD A GOOD FRIEND WHO WAS INTERESTED IN THE RECOVERY OF INDIAN ARTIFACTS. WHEN WE SAW SOME OF HIS COLLECTION OF ARROWHEADS AND POTTERY, BOTH BOB AND I BECAME FASCINATED WITH THIS SUBJECT. HIS FRIEND TAUGHT US HOW TO IDENTIFY FLINT – THE MAIN TYPE OF STONE USED TO MAKE ARROWHEADS. WE STARTED WALKING THE FIELDS ALONG THE DELAWARE RIVER WHEN FARMERS WOULD PLOW IN THE SPRING BEFORE PLANTING CROPS. MANY TIMES WHEN THEY PLOWED THE EARTH, IT WOULD BRING UP ARROWHEADS AS WELL AS ARTIFACTS.

THIS BECAME SUCH AN EXCITING TIME FOR BOTH OF US AND WE HAVE QUITE A COLLECTION OF ARROWHEADS, SPEAR POINTS, BIRD POINTS, SINKERS, AXES AND POUNDING STONES FROM THE LENNI LENAPE INDIAN TRIBE WHO CAMPED ALONG THE DELAWARE RIVER. ADDITIONALLY, OUR CHILDREN LEARNED ABOUT THIS AND OFTEN WALKED THE FIELDS WITH US. ONE TIME, WHEN BOB WAS ON THE CLIFFS OF THE PALISADES ON THE HUDSON RIVER, HE WAS EXPLAINING TO

OUR 7-YEAR-OLD AND 9-YEAR-OLD DAUGHTERS HOW THE CONTINENTAL ARMY PUT SERIES OF CHAINS ACROSS THE HUDSON RIVER TO STOP THE BRITISH SHIPS FROM DIVIDING THE COLONIES, OUR 3 YEAR OLD DAUGHTER SAID "LOOK DADDY, I FOUND AN ARROWHEAD". LOW AND BEHOLD, SHE ACTUALLY FOUND A SMALL BIRD POINT! BOB HAD IT PUT ON A GOLD CHAIN SO THAT SHE WOULD ALWAYS HAVE HER FIND.

COLLECTION OF ARROWHEADS FOUND IN NJ, NY AND PA

CHAPTER 8

POLITICS AND LEGISLATION

AS A LAW ENFORCEMENT OFFICER, BOB FELT THAT IT WAS NOT ONLY HIS DUTY TO UPHOLD THE LAW, BUT ALSO FELT THAT HE SHOULD TAKE AN ACTIVE ROLE IN DEVELOPING LAWS OR CHANGES TO LAW THAT WERE FAIR AND MEANINGFUL.

IN 1970, BOB WORKED WITH THEN ASSEMBLYMAN JOSEPH COSTA PROPOSING A LAW MAKING USE OF COUNTERFIT LICENSES ILLEGAL. ADDITIONALLY, HE PROPOSED AN AMENDMENT TO NEW JERSEY'S POLLUTION BILL. THE ORIGINAL BILL PENALIZED ONLY PASSENGER VEHICLES YET DID NOT INCLUDE THE BIGGEST SOURCES OF POLLUTION (TRUCKS AND BUSES). THE PROPOSED AMENDMENT WOULD NOW HOLD THOSE VEHICLES ACCOUNTABLE TO MEET ANTI-POLLUTION STANDARDS. BOTH THESE PIECES OF LEGISLATURE WERE PASSED.

IN 1973, HE AGAIN PROPOSED ANOTHER BILL, THIS TIME WITH SENATOR DOMINIC RINALDI, MAKING IT ILLEGAL TO USE ANOTHER PERSON'S LICENSE FOR IDENTIFICATION AND DRIVING. IT ALSO PASSED AND SIGNED INTO LAW.

IN 1974, THEN BERGEN COUNTY SHERIFF JOE JOB RECOMMENDED BOB'S APPOINTMENT TO GOVERNOR BYRNES' MOTOR VEHICLE STUDY COMMISSION.

AS A RESULT OF HIS TENURE ON THE COMMISSION, BOB WORKED WITH SENATOR MARASSA TO REVISE THE LAW AND PENALTY FOR DRUNK DRIVING. THE PENALTY WAS INITIALLY TWO YEARS, WHICH RESULTED IN SIGNIFICANT LOSS OF LIVELIHOOD AND FAMILY HARDSHIP AND MORE IMPORTANTLY, DID NOT ADDRESS THE SOURCE OF THE INFRACTION. HE PROPOSED THAT THE DRIVER'S LICENSE SHOULD STILL BE REVOKED, BUT IN ORDER TO REINSTATE THE LICENSE (WITHIN TWO TO SIX MONTHS), THE DRIVER WOULD NEED TO SUCCESSFULLY COMPLETE AND PASS A REHABILITATION PROGRAM (AND HOPEFULLY, PREVENT THE DRIVER FROM DRUNK DRIVING IN THE FUTURE).

IN ADDITION TO LEGISLATION, BOB ALSO HAD AN INTEREST IN SERVING HIS IMMEDIATE COMMUNITY. IN 1978, BOB WAS ELECTED COUNCILMAN FOR HIS HOMETOWN, MAYWOOD, NEW JERSEY. ONE OF THE COUNCIL'S GREATEST ACCOMPLISHMENTS AT THIS TIME WAS THE CONSTRUCTION OF A SENIORS' BUILDING. THIS WOULD ALLOW SENIORS TO LIVE IN THE TOWN THEY LOVED WHEN THEY WERE NO LONGER ABLE TO MAINTAIN THEIR HOMES.

AS DESCRIBED IN A PREVIOUS CHAPTER, BOB RAN AND WON THE ELECTION FOR THE POSITION OF BERGEN COUNTY SHERIFF IN 1987. HE SERVED THE COUNTY FROM 1988 THROUGH 1990.

COMMEMORATIVE PEN FROM LEGISLATION BOB CO-WROTE

ROBERT R. HERB: A MAN OF MANY FACES

CHAPTER 9

THE HUNTSMAN AND NATURE LOVER

BOB'S GREATEST ENJOYMENT WAS WALKING THROUGH THE FIELDS WITH OUR HUNTING DOGS AND SHOOTING PHEASANTS AND GROUSE. IT GAVE HIM COMPLETE QUIET TIME WITH NATURE. OUR DOGS ALSO ENJOYED THIS TIME WITH BOB, RETRIEVING THE BIRDS HE SHOT, AND ENJOYING THE OUTDOORS AS WELL.

BOB WOULD TELL OUR GIRLS HOW WE WERE ABLE TO EAT LIKE KINGS – WHOSE SPECIAL FOOD WAS PHEASANT! MOST PEOPLE TODAY DO NOT HAVE THE OPPORTUNITY TO ENJOY THIS DELICACY. HE WOULD ALSO HUNT ANNUALLY FOR ONE DEER FOR VENISON MEAT. HE WAS A CONCIENTIOUS HUNTER – HE ALWAYS TOLD THE GIRLS THAT ONE SHOULD ONLY SHOOT AN ANIMAL FOR FOOD, NEVER FOR JUST SPORT/KILLING. FAMILY AND FRIENDS ENJOYED THE MEATS BOB HUNTED FOR…ONE THANKSGIVING, WE EVEN HAD A WILD TURKEY!

BOB WAS ALSO A NATURE LOVER. HE WOULD ALWAYS TAKE PITY ON A WILD ANIMAL THAT WAS INJURED OR IN DISTRESS AND TRY TO HELP THEM. FOR EXAMPLE, ONE MORNING AFTER BOB HAD BEEN ON PATROL DURING THE MIDNIGHT SHIFT, I FOUND A BLACKBIRD IN A CAGE IN MY KITCHEN. BOB TOLD ME THAT IT WAS RAINING SO HARD THE NIGHT BEFORE AND HE FOUND THE BIRD ON THE SIDE

OF THE ROAD UNABLE TO FLY OR GET OFF THE ROAD. HE SAID THAT HE WANTED TO LET THE BIRD REST AND DRY AND THAT WHEN THE GIRLS AWOKE IN THE MORNING, THEY COULD HELP HIM RELEASE THE BIRD WHICH THEY DID.

ANOTHER TIME, BOB BROUGHT HOME A PIGEON THAT HAD AN INJURED LEG AND AGAIN COULD NOT FLY OR WALK. THE PIGEON WAS KEPT FOR SEVERAL DAYS IN A CAGE UNTIL SHE HEALED. BECAUSE SHE WOBBLED ABOUT THE CAGE THE FIRST FEW DAYS, THE GIRLS NAMED HER "PEG-LEG". ONCE PEG-LEG HAD HEALED, SHE WAS RELEASED. FOR ABOUT THREE YEARS AFTER, A PIGEON (PEG-LEG?) WOULD RETURN TO OUR HOUSE AND SIT ON TOP OF OUR ROOF. WE ALL THOUGHT THAT SHE WAS COMING FOR A VISIT AFTER WE CARED FOR HER.

ROBERT R. HERB: A MAN OF MANY FACES

CHAPTER 10

FAMILY LEGACY: A HUSBAND, FATHER, GRANDFATHER AND GREAT GRANDFATHER

BOB ALWAYS MADE TIME FOR HIS FAMILY. AS A COUPLE, WE WOULD HAVE A NIGHT OUT FOR DINNER WHEN GRANDMA AND GRANDPA COULD WATCH THE GIRLS. WHEN THE GIRLS GREW UP, WE WERE ABLE TO SPEND MORE TIME TOGETHER TRAVELING TO EUROPE. WE VISITED LONDON, PARIS, SWITZERLAND, HOLLAND, AND GERMANY. WE ALSO TOOK TWO CRUISES – ONE TO BERMUDA AND ANOTHER DOWN THE RHINE RIVER FROM AMSTERDAM TO STRAUSSBERG, GERMANY. WE ALSO VISITED THE PARADISE ISLANDS, STE MAARTEN AND ARUBA.

THE CHILDREN WERE VERY SPECIAL TO BOB. WE ALWAYS ENJOYED SUMMER VACATIONS TOGETHER GOING TO NOVA SCOTIA, NIAGARA FALLS, MONTREAL, TORONTO, AND ONTARIO, CANADA. WE ALSO TOOK THEM TO FLORIDA ON AN OVERNIGHT TRAIN RIDE. HE TAUGHT THE GIRLS HOW TO SWIM, FISH, TARGET SHOOT WITH BB GUNS (UNDER SUPERVISION), AND HOW TO DRIVE A STICK-SHIFT

CAR. HE MADE SURE THEY COULD CHECK THE OIL IN THEIR CARS AND COULD CHANGE A FLAT TIRE IF NECESSARY.

I AM SURE THAT THE GIRLS' SUCCESSES IN THEIR CAREERS AND ADULT LIVES WERE DUE TO THEIR FATHER'S GREAT EXAMPLE. OUR OLDEST DAUGHTER, THERESA, IS A FAMILY NURSE PRACTITIONER. SHE STARTED HER NURSING CAREER IN NEONATAL INTENSIVE CARE AND MADE THE FRONT PAGE OF THE NEWSPAPERS AS ONE OF THE NURSES CARING FOR THE FIRST ONE POUND BABY IN HACKENSACK MEDICAL CENTER. SHE CONTINUED HER EDUCATION AND BECAME A NURSE PRACTITIONER WHO THEN WORKED WITH A NEUROSURGEON AND HIS TEAM CARING FOR CHILDREN AND ADULTS WITH BRAIN AND SPINE ISSUES. IN ADDITION TO HER DAY-TO-DAY ROLE, THERESA AUTHORED SEVERAL CHAPTERS IN PEDIATRIC NEUROSURGICAL NURSING TEXTS, PUBLISHED AN ARTICLE IN A MEDICAL JOURNAL, AND WAS ON VARIOUS LOCAL AND NATIONAL COMMITTEES. SHE HAS DONE NATIONAL PRESENTATIONS TO NEUROSCIENCE NURSES, AS WELL AS TEACHING CLASSES TO STAFF AT SEVERAL HOSPITALS. SHE ALSO HOLDS SEVERAL CERTIFICATIONS IN HER FIELD. DESPITE HER CAREER, SHE IS THE MOTHER OF A DAUGHTER AND TWO SONS.

PATRICIA, OUR SECOND DAUGHTER IS ALSO A NURSE PRACTITIONER (NP) WITH A CERTIFICATION IN ACUTE CARE. IN ADDITION TO HER MASTERS DEGREE IN NURSING, SHE ALSO HAS A SECOND MASTERS DEGREE IN PUBLIC HEALTH. SHE IS A PIONEER IN HER FIELD, DEVELOPING MANY NP-DRIVEN PROGRAMS IN TRAUMA, EMERGENCY MEDICINCE, ORTHOPEDICS, AND SURGERY. HER CAREER BEGAN AT HACKENSACK MEDICAL CENTER WHERE SHE CARED FOR MANY ACUTELY ILL AND INJURED PATIENTS. SHE THEN WENT TO WORK FOR AN ORTHOPEDIC SURGEON AT THE HOSPITAL FOR SPECIAL SURGERY IN NEW YORK CITY. IN 2010 AFTER A 7.0 MAGNITUDE EARTHQUAKE STRUCK HAITI, PATRICIA WAS ASKED TO JOIN AN ORTHOPEDIC TRAUMA TEAM FROM THE HOSPITAL TO PROVIDE CARE FOR THE RESIDENTS OF HAITI. SHE CONTINUES HER PROFESSIONAL MISSION TO IMPROVE BONE HEALTH, A PUBLIC HEALTH PROBLEM, FOR HER PATIENTS WHO HAVE SUSTAINED FRACTURES OR WHO ARE AT RISK FOR A FRACTURE DUE TO LOW BONE MINERALIZATION. SHE CONDUCTS BONE HEALTH LECTURES TO COLLEAGUES AND THE COMMUNITY. SHE HAS PUBLISHED JOURNAL ARTICLES ON BONE HEALTH. SHE IS THE MOTHER OF THREE SONS.

OUR THIRD DAUGHTER, BARBARA, HAS HAD SUCCESS IN THE FINANCIAL FIELD BECOMING VICE PRESIDENT OF PROPERTY MANAGEMENT ACCOUNTING WITH AN INTERNATIONAL BANK. SHE THEN BECAME SENIOR VICE PRESIDENT

OF INVESTMENT ACCOUNTING AND PORTFOLIO OPERATIONS WITH A MAJOR REAL ESTATE INVESTMENT FIRM. AND FINALLY, SHE ASSUMED THE POSITION OF GLOBAL HEAD OF REAL ASSETS WITH A TOP TIER FUND SERVICE PROVIDER. BARBARA HAS BEEN VERY ACTIVE WITHIN THE INVESTMENT REAL ESTATE INDUSTRY THROUGHOUT HER CAREER, HOLDING VARIOUS BOARD POSITIONS AND COMMITTEE CHAIRMANSHIPS THROUGH WHICH MAJOR ACCOMPLISHMENTS INCLUDE GLOBAL ACCEPTANCE OF SEVERAL INDUSTRY STANDARDS. BARBARA HOLDS A BACHELORS DEGREE IN ACCOUNTING AND IS A CPA IN THE STATE OF NEW JERSEY. SHE IS THE MOTHER OF TWO SONS.

BOB ALWAYS MADE TIME FOR HIS EIGHT GRANDCHILDREN – MATTHEW, ANDREW, SEAN, DANIEL, MICHAEL, SHANNON, ROBERT AND BRYAN. WE WOULD ATTEND SCHOOL AND SPORTING EVENTS AND SPEND HOLIDAYS AND BIRTHDAYS WITH THEM. WE EVEN BOUGHT A MINIVAN SO THAT WE COULD BRING THE CHILDREN (AND SOMETIMES A DOG OR TWO) TO OUR COUNTRY HOUSE IN PENNSYLVANIA. THE KIDS WOULD SPEND HOURS CATCHING FROGS AT THE POND BEHIND THE HOUSE. BOB WOULD MAKE THEM NETS TO CATCH THEM AND FILL BUCKETS WITH WATER TO PUT THE FROGS IN. HE WOULD ALSO TAKE THEM BLUEBERRY PICKING AND APPLE PICKING. I WOULD OFTEN MAKE BLUEBERRY PANCAKES FOR BREAKFAST AND IN THE FALL, MADE APPLESAUCE WITH THE APPLES. THEY ALL LOVED TO EAT WHAT THEY PICKED AND STILL, TO THIS DAY, REMEMBER THESE ACTIVITIES.

BOB AND I ARE VERY LUCKY TO BE ABLE TO NOT ONLY HAVE BEEN A PART OF THEIR LIVES AS THEY GREW, BUT NOW ALSO GET TO SEE THEIR CHILDREN. WE CURRENTLY HAVE NINE GREAT GRANDCHILDREN (TAYLOR, COOPER, TYSON, LENNI, CARTER, CAMERON, JULIETTE, FINN, AND AIRI) AND GREAT GRANDBABY NUMBER TEN (A BABY GIRL) IS ON THE WAY.

BOB'S THREE DAUGHTERS

JOAN P. HERB

CHAPTER 11

EDUCATION, AWARDS AND ACHIEVEMENTS

EDUCATION

LINCOLN TECHNICAL SCHOOL – PLUMBING (1958)

BERGEN COMMUNITY COLLEGE – ASSOCIATE DEGREE POLICE SCIENCE (1974)

WILLIAM PATERSON COLLEGE – BACHELOR OF SCIENCE CRIMINOLOGY (1977)

WILLIAM PATERSON COLLEGE – MASTER DEGREE CRIMINOLOGY (1980)

POLICE CAREER

DEPARTMENT OF MOTOR VEHICLES HIGHWAY PATROL 1959-1962

BERGEN COUNTY POLICE PATROLMAN 1962-1976

BERGEN COUNTY POLICE DETECTIVE SARGEANT 1977

BERGEN COUNTY POLICE LIEUTENANT 1982

BERGEN COUNTY POLICE CAPTAIN 1984

BERGEN COUNTY SHERIFF 1988-1990

CERTIFICATIONS FROM BERGEN COUNTY POLICE ACADEMY

PHOTOGRAPHY COURSE 02/07/1964

POLICE ADMINISTRATION COURSE 02/14/1964

SEX CRIMES CERTIFICATION 02/20/1964

INVESTIGATION COURSE 03/06/1964

NJ STATE POLICE CERTIFICATION IN CHEMICAL TESTS FOR INTOXICATION 04/24/1964

CERTIFICATE FOR BREATHALYZER 02/17/1967

CERTIFICATION WEIGHMASTER 05/31/1966

CERTIFICATION ON MOB AND RIOT CONTROL 04/05/1968

CERTIFICATION FOR ALCOHOL AND HIGHWAY SAFETY 05/07/1969

TRAFFIC INSTITUTE NORTHWEST UNIVERSITY ACCIDENT INVESTIGATION COURSE 01/20/1970

BASIC CONVERSATIONAL SPANISH COURSE 01/21/1972

CERTIFICATION IN ORGANIZED CRIME 02/27/1974

CERTIFICATION ON POLICE ROLE AND IMAGE 12/14/1974

POLICE TRAFFIC OFFICERS ASSOCIATION OF BERGEN COUNTY (PTOABC)

BOB REALIZED THAT THERE WAS NO ORGANIZATION OF THE TRAFFIC OFFICERS AND RELATED CIVILIANS IN BERGEN COUNTY AS THERE WERE IN NEIGHBORING COUNTIES IN NEW JERSEY. BOB PROPOSED TO THE VARIOUS POLICE CHIEFS THROUGHOUT BERGEN COUNTY THAT AN ORGANIZATION BE FORMED

SUPPORTING THOSE INVOLVED WITH TRAFFIC SAFETY. UNANIMOUSLY, THE CHIEFS AGREED AND IN 1984, THE PTOABC WAS FORMED. AS PER THEIR MISSION STATEMENT, "THE GOAL OF THE ASSOCIATION WAS TO ORGANIZE POLICE OFFICERS INTO A CENTRAL BODY AND KEEP THEM INFORMED OF THE LAWS, THE LATEST COURT RULINGS, LEGISLATION, TRAINING AND TECHNOLOGY PERTAINING TO TRAFFIC SAFETY".

THE GROUP JUST CELEBRATED THEIR 40TH ANNIVERSARY AND AT THEIR EVENT, THE JOURNAL INCLUDED BOB'S ORIGINAL LETTER SENT TO THE CHIEFS OF POLICE. WHAT A WONDERFUL TRIBUTE TO THE MAN WHO HAD THE CONCEPT AND WHEREWITHALL TO MAKE IT HAPPEN.

Police Traffic Officers Association of Bergen County

40th Anniversary

June 1984 - June 2024

OUR HISTORY

COUNTY OF BERGEN

POLICE DEPARTMENT
66 ZABRISKIE STREET • HACKENSACK, N.J. 07601 • (201) 646-2700

Edward A. Schmalz, Jr.
Chief of Police

January 3, 1984

To: Chief Edward Schmalz
From: Lieut. Robert Herb, Traffic Safety

Subject: Proposal To Chiefs Of Police- Forming Of Traffic Officers Assoc.

Sir:

A request is made through your office to the Bergen County Chiefs Of Police Association to form within this county and organization comprised of traffic officers and related traffic safety individuals to be known as:

"The Bergen County Traffic Officers Association"

Bergen County, with more police departments than any other county, needs such an organization because of the many traffic related problems caused by:

more registered automobiles in Bergen County than any other county
approximately 3000 miles of municipal, county, state roads
projected 1985 census of the county with the highest population
a "corridor" county with a very high rate of traffic to and from New York City
the only county in N.J. with two borders to a state (N.Y.) with 19 yr. drinking

In addition to the problems caused by traffic, is also the problem of frequent changes and additions to the state motor vehicle laws that are not being distributed to our Bergen County departments as they once were through enforcement bulletins sent by the Division Of Motor Vehicles.

A survey of traffic safety officers from various police departments in this county that was conducted by the undersigned, has indicated unanimous support and need for such an organization. A traffic officers association in Bergen County would be similar to other traffic groups in New Jersey as; Monmouth and Union County Traffic Officers Assoc., South Jersey Traffic Officers Assoc., and New Jersey Police Traffic Officers Association. Fanwood Police Chief Anthony Parenti, President of N.J. Police Traffic Officers, in

---

Robert P. Palluita
Director

BOARD OF CHOSEN FREEHOLDERS

Harry J. Gurecki
Deputy Director

Fred Cerbo   Barbara H. Chadwick   Archie F. Hay   Arthur F. Jones   Susanne Knudsen   Doris Mahalick   Richard A. Mola

Page Two

recent conversation with the undersigned has pledged the support and cooperation of his organization to the concept and formation of a traffic officers association in Bergen County.

It is hoped that the Bergen County Chiefs Of Police Association will review this request, and if approved, a liason to such organization be appointed by the chiefs to serve on the executive board of such organization in addition to the forming of this traffic officers association.

Respectfully submitted,

Lieut. Robert Herb, Supervisor
Traffic Safety Division

EPILOGUE

I WOULD FIRST LIKE TO FORMALLY DEDICATE THIS BOOK TO BOB. I HAVE BEEN A WITNESS TO THE MAJORITY OF HIS LIFE ACCOMPLISHMENTS AND HAVE ALWAYS BEEN SO PROUD. IN FACT, WHEN HE BECAME SHERIFF, I HAD A RING DESIGNED FOR HIM TO WEAR COMMEMORATING THE PINNACLE OF HIS LAW ENFORCEMENT CAREER. WHAT HAS BEEN SO AMAZING TO ME IS THAT BOB NOT ONLY EXCELLED IN HIS CAREER AND PROFESSION, BUT ALSO HAD SO MANY INTERESTS THAT HE PURSUED AND ENJOYED THROUGHOUT HIS LIFE. HE HAS ALWAYS SHARED WHAT HE LEARNED AND TOOK SUCH PLEASURE IN SEEING OTHERS USING THEIR "NEW SKILLS". THIS COULD BE SOMEONE CATCHING A FISH, GRAFTING AN APPLE SCION, OR A ROOKIE POLICE OFFICER LEARNING HOW TO BE BETTER AT THE JOB.

SECONDLY, I WANT TO THANK MY GRANDSON ROBERT WITH ALL HIS HELP AND EXPERTISE IN WRITING THIS BOOK. HE HELPED ME WITH PUTTING THE THOUGHTS IN A COMPUTER DOCUMENT AND SCANNED PICTURES AND DOCUMENTS THAT ARE THROUGHOUT THE BOOK. I ALSO WANT TO THANK MY DAUGHTERS FOR READING, EDITING, AND MAKING THIS BOOK PUBLICATION READY.

I HAVE BEEN LUCKY TO BE A PART OF THIS SPECIAL MAN'S LIFE. I HOPE THIS BOOK ALLOWS HIS LEGACY TO CONTINUE WITH HIS CHILDREN, GRANDCHILDREN AND GREAT GRANDCHILDREN.

WITH MUCH LOVE AND ADMIRATION,

JOAN

SHERIFF'S RING DESIGNED BY JOAN FOR BOB

Milton Keynes UK
Ingram Content Group UK Ltd.
UKHW051400011224
451844UK00004B/53